WRECKING BALL

Action Hero

WRECKING BALL

OBERON BOOKS
LONDON

WWW.OBERONBOOKS.COM

First published in 2016 by Oberon Books Ltd
521 Caledonian Road, London N7 9RH
Tel: +44 (0) 20 7607 3637 / Fax: +44 (0) 20 7607 3629
e-mail: info@oberonbooks.com
www.oberonbooks.com

A catalogue record for this book is available from the British
Library.

PB ISBN: 9781786820211
E ISBN: 9781786820228

Cover image by Gemma Paintin and James Stenhouse

Commissioned by the Spring Festivals Commission
2015: Sprint, Watch Out, Mayfest, Pulse
and Latitude Festival. Seeded by greenhouse,
A Farnham Maltings initiative, and developed
with the support of the National Theatre Studio,
The Point, Eastleigh and The West End Centre.
Supported using public funding by the National
Lottery through Arts Council England.

Written, created and performed by
Gemma Paintin and James Stenhouse

Dramaturgy by Deborah Pearson

Produced by Mel Scaffold

Introduction

This might seem strange considering we're theatre makers, but Action Hero are scared of theatre. We're afraid of 'plays'. When we began working together in 2005, our desire to make theatre came from an urge to disrupt and re-imagine the ways in which audiences, authors and performers could meet in the moment of performance. It felt to us like the conventional ways of telling stories on stage could never address the problem of who gets to tell those stories, and whose stories we get to hear.

Our interest instead lay in collaborating *with* our audience rather than doing something *for* them, and so we have created performances for live audiences in every different kind of form imaginable: a DIY stunt show, an imagined western in a bar, a six-hour-long argument to camera, a noise gig that goes wrong, a deconstructed underdog sports movie, a collective uncovering of a miniature city hidden underneath ash. All types of theatre, but never a play. Until now.

So *Wrecking Ball* is our first play. We have always used writing as part of our process, but this is the first time we set out intentionally to write a play. It's also the first time we've created work for an end-on theatre; the stage is set up as it normally would be, without our usual re-configuration disrupting the relationship between the performer and the audience. In *Wrecking Ball*, we're using the theatre space (mostly) in the way it is intended. We were searching for a form that would suit the content of the piece and it seemed right that it be a play. We like to think of *Wrecking Ball* as a site-specific piece for a theatre space.

In that sense, *Wrecking Ball* is about theatre. Or more accurately, it's about make-believe. It's about the seductive qualities of theatre, language and images. It's about the power dynamics that exist in any relationship (including the relationship between an audience and an artist), some of which we can see, some of which are hidden. It's about the wielding of 'soft' power and the ways in which well-meaning people might abuse their positions of power unintentionally. It's also about how power might be intentionally misused under the cover of the word 'artist', and how art itself (or an act of creation) can have a destructive power of its own. What if the moment of creation is simultaneously the moment of destruction? What if images can wreck us while grinning innocently at us through the lens?

So to our minds, *Wrecking Ball* is a kind of 'trojan horse' piece of theatre. It's the work of Action Hero dressed up to look like a conventional play, although the disguise is lightly worn. Gently seeping through the dialogue is the concept-led discourse of two live artists wrestling with form. The costumes are hardly costumes at all, and when the celebrity shouts at the photographer, "are you wearing a fucking costume?!" its hard to know for sure whether he is or he isn't. Is that James up there, in his actual clothes? The performers are performing, there's definitely some acting going on, but we can see the two artists as much as we can see their 'characters'. This duality pervades the piece in multiple ways, and all the objects, the music, the set and the language are not necessarily what they appear to be. There is always a slippage going on, between reality and simulation, between truth and fiction, authenticity and fakery.

On the surface though, *Wrecking Ball* is about a photographer taking a photo of a woman who is probably a celebrity. She wants to be young enough to be hot, but old enough to be *old enough*, and definitely not *old*. She wants to be reinvented, to be for real this time. She looks like every blonde you've ever seen, like the blonde gracing the giant billboard of your imagination, selling you whatever it is you want to believe in. The photographer seems familiar too, in his hipster uniform and with his casual friendliness. And so he begins to photograph her, to shape her and to shape the world around her –and us– to make her into the image inside all our heads.

The photographer in *Wrecking ball* is a stand-in for the creator of a play, be that a writer, artist or author. As he gradually builds a fiction so strong that she eventually has no choice but to play along, despite her misgivings, the play constructs and deconstructs fiction and reality in order to confuse the two so thoroughly that we don't fully know what we are looking at anymore: is that his real shirt? Is that her real cocktail? Are those real beers? The (fake) pineapple in *Wrecking Ball* is a stand-in for a multitude of images and ideas in the same way that actors are stand-ins for real people and in the same way that fiction stands in for reality.

Perhaps it doesn't matter how real you are when you're inside a theatre; whatever you do will always be read as fiction. Even the characters in the play can't escape the inevitable slide back into make-believe.

We see the celebrity in *Wrecking Ball* stuck inside the script, all her attempts to subvert it inevitably appropriated by the author(s) in service of the fiction at the same time as we see any number of real life celebs attempting to show themselves to be different, real, hot, rebellious, new, sexy, reinvented, empowered by acting outside of their own scripts, only to find everything they do reincorporated into a narrative that is inescapable. Or maybe the celebrity in *Wrecking Ball* knew that all along, and all this faux-rebellion is just a way to sell records, and the perfect picture is her weapon of choice.

The engineers of our destruction aren't necessarily going to be those who control the military or the nuclear weapons. Perhaps it more likely that they will be the ones in control of images and the way we 'see' things, of how ideas are communicated and repackaged in order to sell us stuff or tell us stories about how they think we, and the world, 'should' be. Perhaps the assumed good in any act of creativity makes it all the more potent a weapon. Like the photographer in *Wrecking Ball,* it can manipulate us, exploit us and abuse us, and then convince us it was all our idea in the first place.

We recently published a book of our collected works called *Action Plans.* The book explored ways of presenting and documenting performance that emphatically weren't play scripts. But, since *Wrecking Ball* is a play, it seemed fitting that we publish the script. In the same way *Wrecking Ball* is a play in inverted commas, this text is a script in inverted commas. It definitely functions as a play script, and you could stage your own version of this play if you wanted to, using this as a blueprint. However, our interest in *Wrecking Ball* as a piece of work isn't in whether or not the play is remounted by another company, and how another director might serve us, the writers, faithfully through their rendition of this text. Rather, we're interested in how *Wrecking Ball,* as an artwork about fiction, cultural narratives and theatre, is more fully realised when this script is published. A play with a published play script is, for us, the ideal medium for this project.

So we're totally sincere when we tell you that *Wrecking Ball* is a straight-up play about a photographer and a celebrity at a photo shoot. But I wouldn't take our word for it.

**Gemma Paintin and James Stenhouse, August 2016
Action Hero**

A black box theatre. Raked seating, a nice wide stage. The "camera" is the audience. In this text, the names GEMMA and JIM are not names of characters. They are the names of the performers and the writers of this play.

The stage is gently lit, as are the audience. A seat on the end of a row in the audience is a little more brightly lit than the others. A little haze. Two people are on the stage.

Music playing softly in the background, the song is Sleep Walk, by The Ventures.

On stage is a white photographer's backdrop with soft boxes and an umbrella flash. A white stool is placed in the centre of the backdrop, which GEMMA is sat on. Stage right is a cooler, full of beer. Stage left is a small bar, with a neon sign hanging above it. It says "Cocktails and Dreams". JIM is making cocktails. Other objects seen later include a fake pineapple, a fake watermelon slice, a fake cocktail, a cone of strawberry ice cream, a parasol, a fake parrot, a pair of sunglasses, a floor fan and confetti.

The audience enter the space. JIM talks to them as they enter. Throughout the play, he moves between the stage and the seat in the audience.

JIM: Come in sit down, sit anywhere you like. You're the first here. Come in. The rest are on their way. Does anyone want a beer while you wait? Help yourself. Hi. Come in. No rush. We have beer, help yourself, I brought the cooler especially. Do you like the cooler? I love that cooler. It's aluminium, thermo-cooled. Do you like the fan? It's a turbo fan, incase it gets hot in here.

Come in. Everyone else is already here. How do you feel about the lights? I'm thinking it needs to be brighter, what do you think? Can we have it brighter, can I see it at 70? Can I see 80? Nice.

Do you need anything? Can I get you anything before we get into it? Does anyone want a beer? Help yourself. I know there's all these lights and all these people but I just want us to imagine it's me and you hanging out together in my apartment or my studio, you know? It's got to feel like that.

Music fades out.

JIM begins sitting in the audience. He addresses them.

This is good isn't it? You're here! I'm here, we're here, we're all here. We all

made it! Fuck! It's been on the horizon
for like, forever! Like a whatdya call it,
like a storm on the horizon! Except not a
storm, like the opposite of a storm. Like a
fuck knows what. Like a, whatever this is.

Are you comfortable by the way? Sorry
you're all up here. I'm not really into
the chairs. They just set up the wrong
chemistry. For me it's all about being
relaxed and having fun. I'm not into it
if it's going to be a formal thing. Sorry,
I'm a bit overexcited; it's a bit much.
I'm just excited to share this time with
you. Share a drink with you. Have you
grabbed a beer? Grab a beer, honestly.

GEMMA: Can I have a beer?

JIM: Hey, look, that's what it's there for!
            I brought the cooler especially! I just
            want this to feel like we're all in my
            apartment, all in my studio. All hanging
            out together. So just relax and take it
            easy. There's no pressure from me,
            no pressure at all coming from me.

GEMMA: Should I sit back down?

JIM: Hey, there's no should, man. It's not
            about should. This is a collaboration.

I'm pretty chilled, I'm like "whatever happens is what happens". I'm not in control of that. It's like, I create the circumstances and then we jam together.

Listen, I respect you enough to believe that you are absolutely in control of your own...situation.[1]

GEMMA: Are you talking to me?

JIM: I think we're all part of the conversation, right?

Pause.

GEMMA: Do you want me to say something?

JIM: Do whatever you like, that's what I was saying to these guys.

GEMMA: Are they gonna be here the whole time or...?

JIM: Don't worry about them, you'll forget they're even here. They're just here in a kind of back-up sort of way, just to assist me if I need it, you know, help me out. But mostly you won't even know they exist.

---

1   Adapted from a letter by Terry Richardson, published in Huffington Post, March 2014

GEMMA: I am going to sit back down.

JIM: Yeah sitting yeah, or standing. What
            you're doing is fine. Sitting, but in a
            relaxed way. Just be yourself. I like to
            keep things casual.

            I've got some ideas I want to knock back
            and forth with you, see if we're on the
            same wavelength.

GEMMA: What kind of ideas?

JIM: Hey, slow down! Why jump straight in?
            It's been so long in the pipeline we may
            as well get to know each other first.

            I'm guessing this is all familiar to you?

GEMMA: Yeah I'm pretty familiar with this kind of
            thing.

JIM: Well, it's a good idea to put all that aside.
            It's better if none of us are bringing any
            baggage with us, do you understand
            what I'm saying? So we can start with a
            clean slate.

GEMMA: Haven't we started already?

JIM: I'm not really into defining things in
            that way, like, who's to say when we

"start"? Or where the beginning or end
is? I don't like things structured or pre-
planned, I just like going with the flow,
you know? It needs to feel alive and
spontaneous.

GEMMA: Right.

JIM: It's not about boundaries.

Flash.

GEMMA: Oh, I wasn't ready.

JIM: That's cool. It's better if you're
             unprepared.

GEMMA: Really?

JIM: Shoot from the hip.

Flash.

             Things just happen when they happen.

GEMMA: It didn't seem like it was all set up.

JIM: Like what was set up?

GEMMA: All the equipment, the lights.

JIM: Yeah, I don't care about that stuff. Lighting, costumes, whatever. I want to just hang out and make some ideas happen, just me and you.

GEMMA: It's just, I thought we were just talking.

JIM: We are! We're just hanging out, having a conversation.

Like, we're just in a dialogue. And when I say that I don't mean "dialogue", I mean we're just talking. For real. This is really happening, right now.

Flash.

See? Think of it more like a spontaneous series of events, none of us know what those events are going to be. We're just letting it flow, and the lights and all the scenery and everything else, that's just all there. Doesn't affect what this is. Yeah? It's just us.

GEMMA: And them.

JIM: Forget about them. I want to just spend some time in a room together and learn new things. Let's get to know each other! Shall we have some music?

GEMMA: Sure.

JIM: What kind of music do you like?

GEMMA: Well, I listen to a lot of different kinds of stuff. All different kinds of music.

JIM: Nice, yeah, cool, like different genres, different eras?

GEMMA: Yeah, like Eighties sometimes.

JIM: And Seventies?

GEMMA: Yeah sometimes Seventies.

JIM: Like Seventies punk? So you listen to punk and things like that?

GEMMA: Is this right? It doesn't feel very spontaneous to me.

JIM: Look, just go with it okay, I know it feels weird but just go with it. We've just got to loosen up. Which bands do you like?

GEMMA: I would say, I mean, I don't specifically like any one band.

JIM: Oh, like you're not really like a fanboy obsessive kind of person. You're like a magpie kind of person, like you don't

have specific loyalties, you're just free to
pick and choose what you like?

GEMMA: Yeah.

JIM: Like Seventies punk, early hip hop,
Nineties rave, J-pop.

GEMMA: Yeah, I like all those things.

JIM: So you're keen to please?

GEMMA: Am I?

JIM: I hope not.

GEMMA: No.

JIM: You don't care what I think.

GEMMA: No. I don't give a shit what you think.

JIM: You don't give a fuck.

GEMMA: I literally don't give a fuck what you think.

Flash.

JIM: That's great, I can work with that.

GEMMA: You think?

JIM: What do you think?

Pause.

GEMMA: I want to do, not think.

JIM: Exactly. Exactly that.

JIM: So, you're angry.

GEMMA: Yeah.

JIM: You want to fight against something.

GEMMA: Definitely.

JIM: What?

GEMMA: Whatever.

JIM: What's your real age?

GEMMA: Uh…

JIM: Your actual age

GEMMA: I don't know what you're asking me here.

JIM: It's a simple question.

Pause.

GEMMA: I'm 35.

JIM: Jesus, God no not you, not your real age –

GEMMA: What, younger?

JIM: Obviously. You're as young as you feel.

GEMMA: 19?

JIM: That's ambitious.

GEMMA: Yeah, okay, I thought we were having
           some music?

JIM: Yes. Perfect. You'd be like, fuck it let's
           dance.

Music plays. Caravan by The Ventures.

GEMMA: I never said I was going to dance.

JIM: So you can just relax, act natural.
           Just move. Naturally.

GEMMA: I can't dance to this.

JIM: Yeah that'll work. You're reluctant.

GEMMA: What is this song? It's terrible.

JIM: Okay, let's do it like that –

GEMMA: Can we try a different piece of music?

JIM: – like we're both messing around and you're talking to me and you're saying something like you would say to me, like "oh come on, stop goofing around okay."

GEMMA: This is ridiculous.

JIM: Yeah perfect like "stop goofing around" yeah.

GEMMA: Stop goofing around, okay!

JIM: That's the sort of thing you'd say and then you'd probably, like, give me the finger.

Yeah but to the camera.

Yeah that's exactly right but just the one finger.

Perfect and you'd probably be laughing, like cheeky, naughty laughing.

GEMMA: I can only laugh if you say something funny.

JIM: Okay, well that's got to be spontaneous. It can't be pre-planned, it won't work that way.

GEMMA: Just say something then.

JIM: Let's just say I say something funny, because that's what I'd probably be doing anyway and then you laugh because that's how you would respond and then you're giving me the finger and then you would probably say something like –

GEMMA: I just want to be myself.

JIM: Oh okay, the real you. So now you're for real.

GEMMA: Yeah, oh yeah I'm the real me now. I want to be the opposite of before.

JIM: You're serious.

GEMMA: I'm me, and I'm totally serious about it.

JIM: But you're playful.

GEMMA: Oh yeah, no yeah I'm still fun. I'm still like "hey yeah I'm the life and soul, not down with that grown up shit" but not a child either.

23

JIM: Children aren't sexy.

GEMMA: I'm not a sexy kid.

JIM: But youth is sexy.

GEMMA: Yeah, oh yeah I'm still young. I'm old
                enough, obviously, but I'm not old.

Music fades out.

JIM: Okay, here's what we're gonna do. I'm
                going to start again and we'll set it up
                like we're doing a stupid interview thing,
                but we're not serious, right? We're just
                pretending. I'll ask you stupid questions.

                What kind of music do you like?

GEMMA: I like all different kinds of stuff. Seventies
                punk, early rave, Nineties hip hop, J pop.
                I'm not really a fangirl kind of person I'm
                more like a magpie kind of person,
                I pick and choose what I like

JIM: Whose your favourite movie star?

GEMMA: Tom Cruise! He's kind of old school, and
                I like that.

JIM: He's creepy, try another.

GEMMA: Patrick Swayze! He's kind of old school,
          and I like that.

JIM: He's dead, I don't think we want that
          association.

GEMMA: He is not dead.

JIM: He is. Death isn't a place we want to go.

GEMMA: Well we're all gonna die, you know?

JIM: Yes but not now, so leave that one alone.

GEMMA: I can't believe he's dead.

JIM: What's your favourite colour?

GEMMA: Pink.

JIM: Too obvious.

GEMMA: Purple.

JIM: Prince owns purple.

GEMMA: Black.

JIM: Black's not a colour.

GEMMA: Yeah it is, it's my favourite colour.

JIM: It's not a colour. It's an absence of light.
                    It's nothing. It's a void.

GEMMA: Okay then, so I'm a void.

JIM: Let's think about it more as a blank
                    canvas.

GEMMA: Well that would be white

JIM: Okay, this isn't working for me right now
                    so let's take a break. Let's have a drink.

*Music plays. Red Sails in the Sunset by Takeshi Tarauchi and
The Bunnys*

Pause.

                    So. Imagine a picture of an egg.
                    What's it about?

GEMMA: Chickens?

JIM: Okay, but what else?

GEMMA: Farming?

JIM: Not really, but what else?

GEMMA: Breakfast?

JIM: Okay, no.

It's about fertility. Femininity. Being a woman, see? When I take a photo of you, it's also a photo of something else. It's a photo of a dream, it's a photo of a nightmare, it's a photo of an entire fucking system.

It's a photo of all of us. Okay?

GEMMA: I think I'm more of a dream than a nightmare, like a wet dream, or a daydream or –

JIM: Right, but what I'm saying is that pictures are a kind of language, and we can use that language to tell a certain story about you.

Imagine it's a tight shot. No bells, no whistles, no photoshop, no make up, no anything. Totally stripped back. No object, no subject, it's a non-concept. It's just the light on the film.

The light travels from the sun and it illuminates the blackness. A flash from the beginning of time! We catch it and we preserve it. The shutter opens and the particles flood in, a thousandth of a second but they stay there forever.

Flash.

JIM puts a pineapple in the backdrop.

What do you see?

GEMMA: A pineapple.

JIM: Look closer. What are we looking at?

Pause.

GEMMA: I can just see a pineapple.

JIM: That's fine, you just need to see it from a different perspective.

Tell me what you see now.

GEMMA: Fruit.

JIM: Give me more.

GEMMA: Spiky fruit, tropical fruit.

JIM: Okay, but what's happening?

GEMMA: Nothing's happening, it's just sitting there.

JIM puts the pineapple on the stool.

JIM: What about now?

Pause.

              Get closer

Pause.

GEMMA: I can see…a pineapple.

JIM: Show me the pineapple.

Pause.

              No. Show me the pineapple!

Pause.

              What am I looking at?

GEMMA: Me with the pineapple.

JIM: Right. Think of an image you've seen
              hundreds of times.

              There's action, it's raw. Something of
              significance is happening right there in
              front of us.

GEMMA: What, like an explosion?

JIM: Is that what I'm looking at?

GEMMA: Uh, is it a grenade?

            A grenade going off?

JIM: Okay. What else?

GEMMA: A gun.

            A man with a gun.

            A man with a gun to his head.

JIM: Good, more!

GEMMA: Blood.

JIM: Yes, where's the blood?

GEMMA: On the sand.

JIM: Where else?

GEMMA: Blood is on the concrete.

JIM: Good, keep going.

GEMMA: Blood on the back seats of cars.

JIM: Yes! Perfect. Something real.

What else?

GEMMA: Warships.

JIM: Incredible.

GEMMA: Warplanes!

JIM: Unbelievable.

GEMMA: Napalm, children running –

JIM: More! More of that!

GEMMA: Helicopters, storm clouds –

JIM: Yes, it's just light on the film!

GEMMA: A famine, a massacre, a huge chasm
            opened up in the ground –

JIM: It's you! That's you!

GEMMA: Tanks!

JIM: What are they doing?

GEMMA: Tanks destroying walls! Tanks destroying
            people! Vultures!

JIM: Hurricanes, earthquakes.

We take hold of that moment. We find that realness for you!

So, what's your message?

GEMMA: There is no message.

JIM: If you had just one message to pass on, what would it be?

GEMMA: The message is, buy the album.[2]

JIM: That's not going to work. Try something else.

GEMMA: There is no message, it's just me.

JIM: That's how you want to do it? Let's do it that way then, I can work with that.

Go from the top, I'll ask you what your message is and you'll say there is no message.

GEMMA: I already said that.

JIM: So say it again, to the camera

GEMMA: That's not who I am anymore. I'm doing it for real or I'm not doing it.

2   Adapted from an interview with Miley Cyrus by Holly Fraser, published in Hunger Magazine, June 2015

JIM: So that's the message?

GEMMA: There is no message, there's just me.

JIM: Okay, let's go back to the beginning.

GEMMA: Right back to the very start?

JIM: We're going back to before anything
            existed, that's where we start.

            We make a space with nothing. And we
            wait, in the nothingness, in the darkness.

            And then, from nowhere, a tiny pin
            prick of light. A microscopic pulsing of
            energy. And it starts expanding, getting
            bigger and bigger until it's all we can
            see. Until you're all we can see. You're
            the light, all the stars in the sky, you're
            the origin of the fucking universe, see?
            And as soon as we see you, we realize
            that everything that came before was just
            primordial soup, formless unstructured
            goop, a fucking vacuum. But the sight of
            you, it's like atoms hurling themselves
            together. Whole worlds are created,
            right? Seeing you is like a supernova,
            an atomic act of divine creation, the big
            bang!

GEMMA: So I'm starting it?

JIM: You're starting the party, cos you're a
          party girl right?

GEMMA: I'm bringing the good times.

JIM: You're bringing all the times.

          You're bringing all of time!

GEMMA: I'm everything that's ever happened,
          and everything that is to come.

JIM: We want to capture that moment.
          The moment life began. We catch it
          and we preserve it. Light particles
          travel through space to get here, they
          make blue for your eyes and red for
          your mouth, they gather above your
          cheekbones and the gap between your
          lips is left alone, like a miniature black
          hole. An event horizon. A flash in the
          dark.

          It's universal. It's iconic.

          Cos we know it's you, right? It's all about
          you and in some ways we want nothing
          else, but we also want everything else,
          do you know what I mean?

So imagine it: a pacific atoll. Palm trees, coconuts, white sands.

GEMMA: Isn't that a bit done?

JIM: It's totally done, that's the point. You're in a bikini, it's sexy, that's a given, you're drinking from a coconut. Tropical.

GEMMA: Okay but behind me, yeah, out to sea, there's a big fucking mushroom cloud.

JIM: Woah. Cool.

So we see the done thing, the cliché and then we fucking blow it to pieces. We see a flash. A huge cloud, there's a sexy delay and then woooooooosh! The palm trees are bent right over, it's like a nuclear wind and it's blowing the bark off the trees, and the sand, and the water, and like fish and pineapples are like flying past you, and boats and you're just letting it blow past. It doesn't even touch you.

GEMMA: Boats?

JIM: Like a yacht or something yeah. We can probably get a picture from hurricane Katrina or the tsunami and then just Photoshop it in and it can fly right past you. Blinding light, eclipsing everything.

So this nuclear blast, it's blowing it all away. It's destroying everything and we're left with just you.

GEMMA: On a beach?

JIM: Yeah, beaches are cool. But maybe it blows the beach away too, maybe it blows everything away so it's just you left.

GEMMA: In a bikini.

JIM: A pacific atoll.

GEMMA: A mushroom cloud.

JIM: Doesn't get anymore iconic than the motherfucking A bomb.

Now, show me the pineapple.

Pause.

JIM: And let's have some music.

Music plays. Beyond the Reef by The Ventures.

GEMMA poses, JIM brings out different objects for her to hold. The flash fires. The final object is an ice cream.

Music fades out.

JIM: No. Something's missing.

                  I'm looking and I'm just seeing you
                  and the ice cream. And what I really
                  want to see is danger or destruction or
                  apocalypse or radical protest or death.

GEMMA: I can do that.

JIM: Okay, let's see danger.

      Flash.

                  Okay destruction?

      Flash.

                  Okay apocalypse.

      Flash.

                  Radical protest.

      Flash.

                  Death?

      Flash.

                  Okay. I'm just not seeing any other
                  layers, I'm just seeing ice cream. It

should hit like a bomb, it should be
explosive.

GEMMA: Explosive.

JIM: It should be like a grenade going off.

GEMMA: So, I'm just minding my business and
           then –

JIM: FLASH! BOOM! Exactly, an explosion.

           You're the big bang! You're atomic
           energy, the creator and the destroyer!

           Go.

Pause.

           Okay. Look.

           After they tested those nukes in the
           desert all the water in the taps went
           brown for like, hundreds of miles.
           Do you see what I'm saying?

           You're the nuke. Everything was clear
           and now it's fucked, nobody knows who
           they are anymore and that's a gift you're
           giving us. You muddied the water, see?

Okay, go.

Pause.

Okay I'm just not seeing it. Nothing's happening.

Pause.

Close your eyes. Close your eyes. What can you see?

GEMMA: I can see a mushroom cloud.

JIM: Great. What else?

GEMMA: I can see the light, and a pacific atoll. A bikini, bikini atoll.

JIM: Nice, give me more of that.

GEMMA: I can see bombs. Big, dick-shaped bombs.

JIM: Perfect, keep going.

GEMMA: I can see the pictures they would draw on the bombs. You know, women in bikinis, and they'd write 'I love you mom' on the side, and maybe I'm the girl on the side of the bomb and it's not 'I love you mom' it's me they love. Maybe we drop these bombs everywhere. Maybe our job is to drop bombs on cities with my name on them and my picture in a bikini.

JIM: Like photo bombs? That's nice.

GEMMA: No, I'm literally saying let's drop bombs on cities with my name on. Let's cause explosions, let's destroy buildings, totally fucking smash cities with my image.

We just have to make sure it's my name on the side of the bomb, and you're like the pilot in the airplane, and you're pressing the big red button.

JIM: Wait. This is really fucking cool.

Do that again, but with more energy. And let's have some music.

Music plays. Teen Beat by The Surfaris.

GEMMA: Okay, okay, right.

I was saying bombs. I was saying let's cause explosions, I was saying let's clear away everything that's gone before so we can rebuild in my image.

Let's destroy buildings, let's smash
cities, let's tear it all down, raze it to the
fucking ground so we can create new
foundations and I'm the new foundation.

Total destruction and reconstruction,
post war, post apocalypse and then
there's me. And I'm the creator and I'm
the destroyer. Nothing has existed before
me and nothing will exist after, I'm the
new history and in that moment, when
we unleash my image onto the world
there'll be light and heat and wind and
it'll be like being reborn –

JIM: Keep it going, it's great! Can we get
some sidelight?

GEMMA: – the whole world, fresh, starting anew!
And we start from me. I'm everything.
There's no meaning except me, there's
no message except me so I'm the perfect
messenger.

I want complete carnage, I want total
devastation, I want to stop time like
there's no before and no after. I want
to embed my image on the retinas of
everyone –

JIM: Keep going, this is great! Can we have
the music louder?

GEMMA: – the entire human race with my image
on their eyeballs! Just one big flash
and then that's all we ever see again,
everything after that in my image, no
history, no future just one long party
in the rubble dancing to my tune, like
I am the bomb and I am the aftermath
and it's bomber jets flying over pacific
islands, dropping bombs with my name
on them, a picture of me in a bikini and
it's cities –

JIM: Eat the ice cream! Eat the ice cream!

GEMMA: – full of people destroyed by my image
I am the beginning and the end I am the
destroyer of worlds I am the destroyer of
worlds!

Flash.

Flash.

JIM: Yes, amazing, that's it!

Death, collapse, apocalypse, sex! It's all
there, you're doing it!

GEMMA: This isn't ice cream!

Music fades out.

JIM: I have literally no idea what you're
          talking about.

GEMMA: This isn't ice cream!

JIM: Do you wanna take five? I'd be happy
          just to take a break for a while.

GEMMA: This ice cream is not a pacific island.

          It's not a beach.

          This ice cream is not a hydrogen bomb.

JIM: It is those things. It's the beach it's the
          sand, sexy, innocent. It's colourful and
          youthful but it's also phallic, like the
          bomb. And it drips, so it's even sexier.

          And we're gonna shoot with it all over
          your face and on your t-shirt and on the
          floor so it is an explosion.

GEMMA: What are you talking about? You're
          talking in fucking code, I don't know
          what you're saying anymore.

          Where are the palm trees, where's the
          bikini, where's the ocean?

This ice cream is not a mushroom cloud. This ice cream isn't even an ice cream!

JIM: It is those things. It's a metaphor for those things.

GEMMA: I haven't used metaphors since like three years ago! Metaphors are dead. The old me was into metaphors, the new me is straight up and for real. You know what for real means? It means no metaphors.

This shoot was supposed to be about making waves.

JIM: We are absolutely making waves

GEMMA: Where? Where are the waves, I don't see any waves. There's no sea, there's no beach. I can't dance on the beach if there is no beach.

It's not a pacific island, it isn't an ice cream and you're a fucking arsehole.

JIM: I don't understand what's upsetting you so much. Do you need a drink of water or something? I can get you some water, or some beer? Or something else?

GEMMA: Can you get me a pacific island?

Pause.

Then screw you! Screw you and your
shitty photo shoot that isn't even a photo
shoot, and your living room which isn't
even a living room, and your camera
which isn't even a camera.

I bet you're not even a photographer.
You're just some prick who thinks it's
cool to pretend he's a photographer. You
think it's cool to just put on a flannel shirt
and skinny jeans and say you're an artist.

Tell them about the ice cream.

JIM: I have no idea what you're talking about.

GEMMA: I bet that's not even your shirt, is it?

Are you wearing a costume? Are you
wearing a fucking costume?

This isn't even a real ice cream.
It's mashed potato! Why is the ice
cream mashed potato?

JIM: It isn't mashed potato.

GEMMA: How come it isn't melting?

45

JIM: It isn't mashed potato.

GEMMA: Eat it then.

JIM: Okay.

GEMMA: Go on, eat the mashed potato and tell
                me it's ice cream.

JIM: Mmmm, strawberry ice cream! I love
                strawberry ice cream

GEMMA: This isn't Los Angeles is it?

JIM: It is, in a way.

GEMMA: He's full of shit, it's mashed potato with
                pink food dye in it!

                You're a liar. I don't believe the words
                you're saying, I don't believe the words
                I'm saying either. I don't believe any of it.

JIM: No one's bothered.

GEMMA: I'm bothered.

JIM: Yeah, well, you're making yourself look
                like an idiot.

GEMMA: No, you're really wrong about that and you know you're wrong about that because it's you who's making me look like an idiot, and I'm not an idiot. I just want to be believable or relatable, I don't want to be a fake.

JIM: You can be whatever you want to be.

GEMMA: Now you know that isn't true.

JIM: Who cares about truth, no one gives a shit.

GEMMA: You know who gives a shit? They give a shit.

JIM: No, they don't, they really don't.

GEMMA: They do! They care! They care about what happens, they care about what it means. These guys are the only real thing in here.

GEMMA sits in the audience seat.

JIM: Eurgh, you're making me feel sick.

GEMMA: It's the mashed potato making you feel sick.

JIM: It's not mashed potato, it's strawberry ice cream.

GEMMA: You just keep trying to believe that until you vomit.

JIM: I don't have to try.

Pause.

GEMMA: We can just sit and chat can't we?

JIM: They won't answer you.

GEMMA: Why not?

JIM: Because it's not in the script.

GEMMA: Let's just sit together and talk like normal human beings in a room. We can do that, can't we?

                  They can't even answer! It's like I don't exist!

JIM: They're trying to be inconspicuous.

GEMMA: Okay. Fine. Fine. Here's the script.

GEMMA holds up this script.

We're right here on page 49.

Anyone? Anyone? See where we are?

Can you see that? It's in yellow. Can you see where to read from?

AUDIENCE: MEMBER

Do you want me to read it?

GEMMA: Yep, you read it. That's what's happening now.

AUDIENCE: MEMBER

I didn't expect to have to do any acting

JIM: Listen buddy, no one here is doing any acting.

GEMMA: Don't listen to him. He's not part of this anymore. We're just going to chat and connect in a genuine way. I want you to feel relaxed, I want you to feel at home here. I know there's all these lights and all these people but I just want us to imagine it's me and you hanging out in my apartment or my studio. We're just having fun, getting to know each other.

Why don't you tell me a bit about yourself?

AUDIENCE:
MEMBER

What do you want to know?

GEMMA:

What do you think of this guy's work? You can be honest with me.

AUDIENCE:
MEMBER

I'm not familiar with it.

GEMMA:

Ha! He's not familiar with your work.

Pause.

What made you come along tonight?

AUDIENCE:
MEMBER

Well, I've been here a few times and I had an okay time so I thought, why not?

GEMMA:

And how is this measuring up? To previous visits I mean?

AUDIENCE:
MEMBER

I think I should probably reserve judgment until it's finished.

GEMMA:

Hmmm. Good answer.

Does this feel like real dialogue to you?

AUDIENCE:
MEMBER

Neither of us sounds particularly convincing.

GEMMA: You know what? I don't think we're the
          problem. Everything sounds fake, even
          you, and you're totally for real.

JIM: Okay, this isn't working for me right now.
          Let's just take a break, let's have some
          music.

Music plays. Maggot Brain by Funkadelic.

          I don't want to bust anyone's balls. Let's
          have a few drinks, let's just hold off for a
          bit, have a beer.

          This is all new for you, I'm throwing a lot
          at you and you're freaking out. I get it.

          Let's just take it easy. Let's have some
          music and some beers and some fucking
          ice cream. Everyone loves ice cream.
          This party needs ice cream.

Pause.

          If you want to dance, you can just dance.
          I'm not going to take any pictures, no
          one's watching.

          I'm not reading from the script anymore,
          the script is bullshit. Let's get what we
          really came for, let's just cut to the chase.

GEMMA: Are you talking to me?

JIM: I'm talking to everyone. Everyone loves
                dancing, everyone loves ice cream.

JIM eats the whole ice cream.

Music fades out.

                So you're not talking to me now? Really?
                You just want to sit there, forever, in
                silence? Because I can't do this without
                you. Nothing happens without you.

Pause.

                I've got something over here you might
                like. Don't you like ice cream?

Pause.

                What do you want? You can have
                whatever you want. Let's just go with the
                flow, come on. You're so good at this.
                You're so good you're making me beg.
                I think we're really getting somewhere
                and that's down to you.

Pause.

Why don't you come over here and
enjoy this delicious ice cream?

Pause.

I love this rebellious spirit, it's what
makes you so special. You don't
conform, I get that. I'm not interested
in the kinds of people who just do what
they're told, I like your anti-authority,
it's fucking cool. I feel like that's why
we connect. Because we're both pushing
against things. That's why we're gonna
make something incredible together.

Come on, come and dance with me. The
sand will feel so soft between your toes.
Come down here and sit on the beach
with me.

The ocean.

You're not the girl who sits things out.
I know you. You don't pass on things
like this. If we want cool stuff to happen
in our lives we have to be open, you
know? We have to be like an open
book. I had so much fun when I was
your age because I was always like,
yes, to whatever anyone said. I still am,
I'm just, yes, to everything. There's

so much no stuff in this life, everyone always saying no, authority and fucking systems just blocking incredible things from happening but you're a yes person, like me. If we say yes in our lives then amazing things come our way.

And I know you like strawberry ice cream. I know you like the beach, I know you like dancing. And it's warm. It's lovely and warm. You're not a backseat kind of person, I know you. You're about being free. Doing whatever you want, having a good time.

Let's dance, let's chill together, eat ice cream and drink mojitos.

Pause.

The sun's about to set. The water's warm, the stars are coming out. Don't you want to see that?

Are you going to miss it because you're sulking?

GEMMA: I'm not sulking.

JIM: No, no, you're just taking it all in. I see you, you look beautiful. You're relaxed,

you're confident. Your hair looks great.
You're the girl.[3]

The dust is settling from the explosion,
it's gonna make the sunset amazing. We
can sit together on the beach and watch
the sun go down.

It's all here, anything you want.

GEMMA comes back onto the stage.

Music plays. Home by The Ventures.

Sunset.

This is what it's all about. You and
me. Just chatting. Together. Relaxed.
Opening up. Allowing ourselves to be
vulnerable, you know? Letting there be
silence. That's how people see the real
you. What's buried underneath. And it's
beautiful. Inside you is beautiful.

GEMMA: You think?

JIM: I know. I can see what's underneath.
            And we've got to show them that
            realness.

---

3   Adapted from an interview with Dov Charney by Claudine Ko, published in
     Jane Magazine, June 2004

When we strip everything back, what are
we left with? We're left with you.
We really see you, for the first time.

GEMMA: But what about the bomb, and the
          mushroom cloud?

JIM: That's all it is. It's the explosion, and
          afterwards, you're what's left. The bomb,
          it blew everything away.

GEMMA: I'm cold.

JIM: It's not cold it's warm.

GEMMA: But if the sun's going down?

JIM: It's humid here. We're in the tropics.
          It stays warm at night.

          Isn't this the most incredible sunset
          you've ever seen? The particles get
          scattered across the wavelengths from
          the sun, the blue gets filtered out and
          all that's left is red and orange. But it's
          beautiful.

GEMMA: Yeah, it is.

JIM: You made that.

GEMMA: Did I?

JIM: Sure.

GEMMA: What happened after the explosion?

JIM: Everything changed in an instant. There
              was a flash, the brightest light you've
              ever seen. And for a moment, one
              perfect moment, just silence and light.

              Then impact, and you're running, and
              everything disappears. It all turns to dust
              around you. Your clothes are ripped
              from your body and your skin is torn
              to pieces and underneath we can see
              pink flesh, and muscle and sinew and
              tissue and then your bones. Pure white
              under the redness. Your ribcage, like a
              cathedral for the most precious part of
              you. And your ribcage is obliterated and
              underneath is your heart. Your heart,
              beating. Everything is blown away and
              we can see your heart on the beach.
              Your beautiful heart. We watch your life
              flash before your eyes, the last heartbeat.

GEMMA: Am I dead?

JIM: You're reborn, new to the world, fresh.
              We see beneath the surface.

              All these things, these material things,
              they don't define you now. Your

sunglasses, your bikini, it doesn't define you. It's not you. We've gone beyond that. We can see the real you now.

GEMMA: My heart.

JIM: That's what we capture.

GEMMA: This is it?

JIM: Yes, it's perfect.

You slowly peel back the layers.
Peel back the bikini, we see you.

GEMMA: What should I be –

JIM: You peel back the bikini. You peel back your bikini so we can see you.

GEMMA: I'm not wearing a bikini.

JIM: You are. You are wearing a bikini. You're eating an ice cream. On the beach. The sun is setting and you're in your bikini.

GEMMA: I'm not wearing a bikini.

JIM: We're on the beach and you're wearing your bikini. But you take it off.

GEMMA: I don't know.

JIM: Look at the sunset. It's called a Rayleigh scattering, the way the particles hit the light from the sun. That's why we see orange and red because the sun is far away from us.

                   The stars are coming out. We're on the beach and you're wearing your bikini. But you take it off. That moment. Totally real, totally perfect.

Music fades out.

                   The water laps the shore and it washes the blood away. And the tide takes you back, back where we all came from, back to nothing. Nothing left.

                   Just the light, making the beach, the sand, the sky, the ocean. That's the moment.

GEMMA takes off an imaginary bikini.

Flash.

Flash.

Flash.

Explosions.

By the same author

**Action Plans: Selected Performance Pieces
by Action Hero**
9781783195008

www.ingramcontent.com/pod-product-compliance
Ingram Content Group UK Ltd.
Pitfield, Milton Keynes, MK11 3LW, UK
UKHW031250020325